I can do my money

Written by Debbie Green

Illustrated by Richard Johnston

How to use this book…

1) Answer the money sums

2) Find the smallest number of coin stickers you can use to answer each question

3) Fill in the spaces

4) If you want to do a sum twice, wipe the answer clean and try again

Draw a line to match the coins to the correct amount. The first one has been done for you.

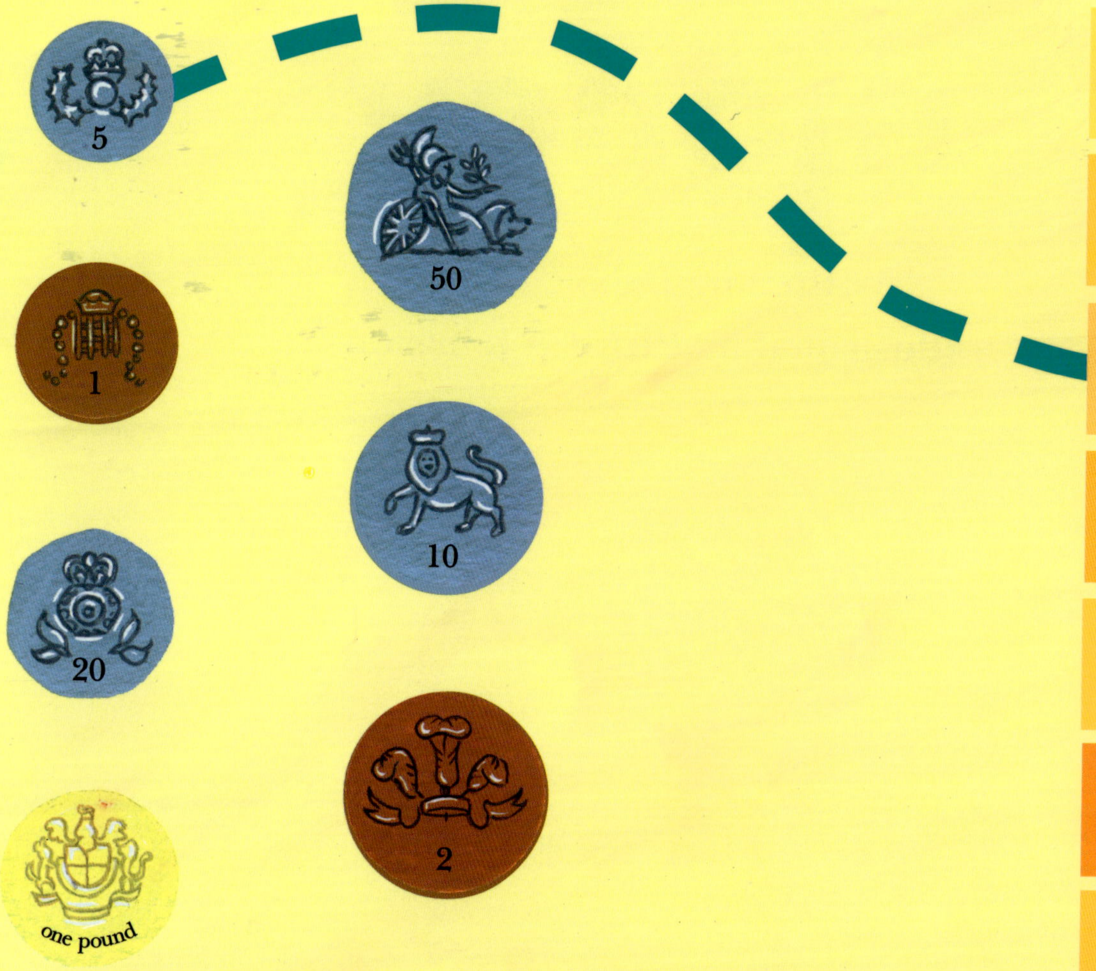

- 1p
- 2p
- 5p
- 10p
- 20p
- 50p
- £1

Write the amount in words.

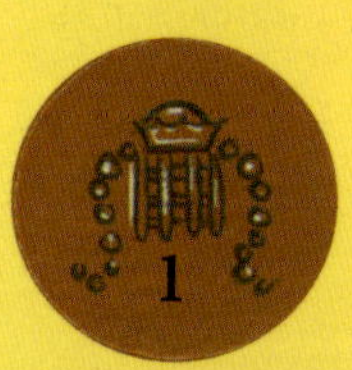

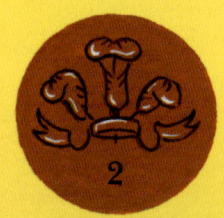

Find coin stickers to answer each money sum.

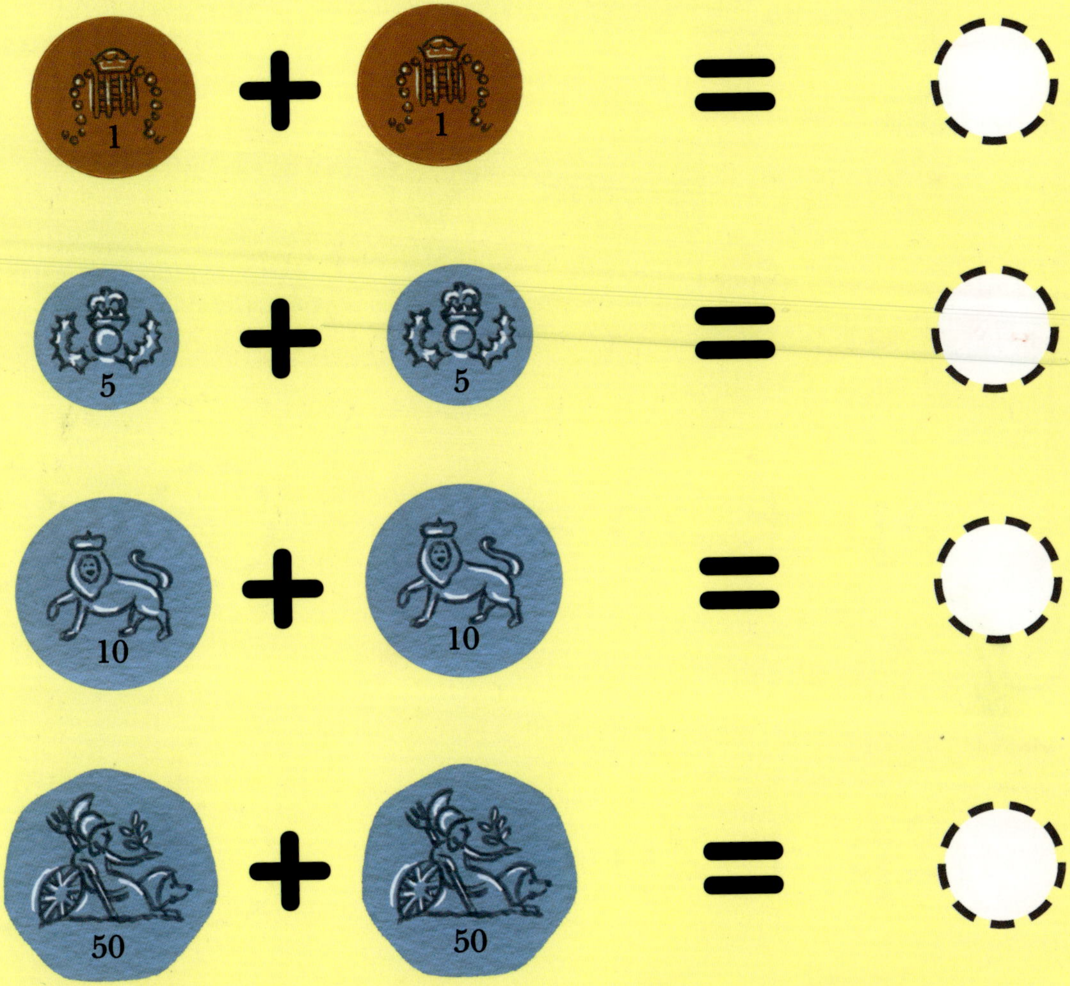

1 + 1 = ◯

5 + 5 = ◯

10 + 10 = ◯

50 + 50 = ◯

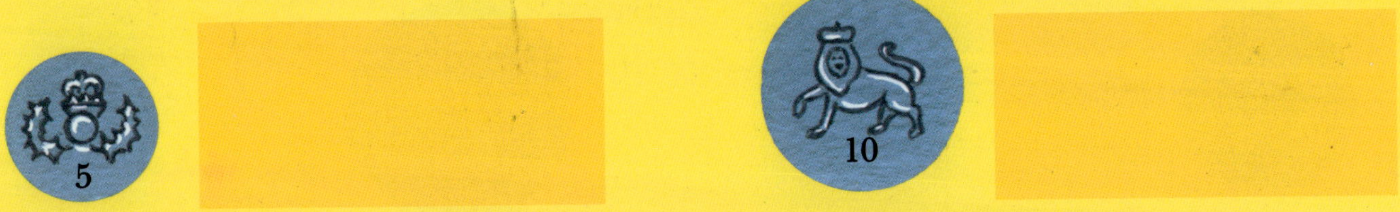

Write the cost of each pair of sweets. Then find coin stickers to make up that amount.

3p

2p

3p + 3p = ☐ ◯ ◯

2p + 2p = ☐ ◯ ◯

Write the amount in words.

 5p + 5p =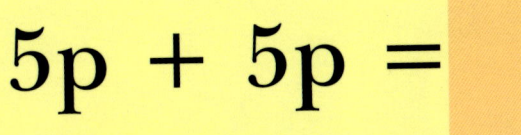

 6p + 6p =

Look at the price labels and find the right coins to buy each thing.

Complete these sums.

£1 + £1 =   50p + 10p =

50p + 5p =   50p + 20p =

Look at the price labels and find the right coins to buy each toy.

Complete these sums.

50p + 50p =   50p + 5p =

50p + 20p + 10p =   £1 + £1 =

You have 10p. Write how much change you get when you buy these things.

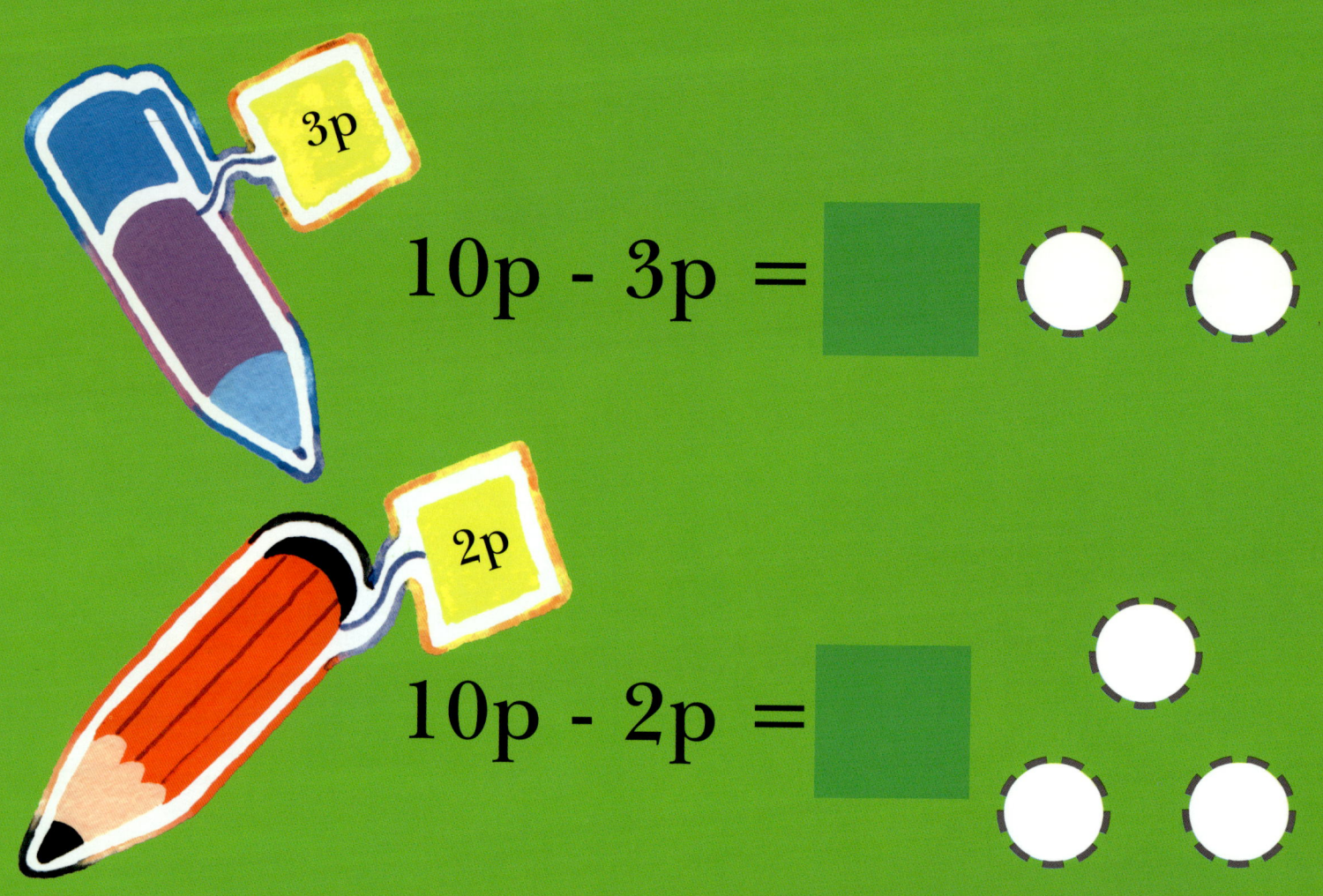

10p - 3p =

10p - 2p =

Complete these sums.

10p - 3p =   10p - 2p =

Find some sticker coins to make up the amount of change that the shopkeeper gives back to you.

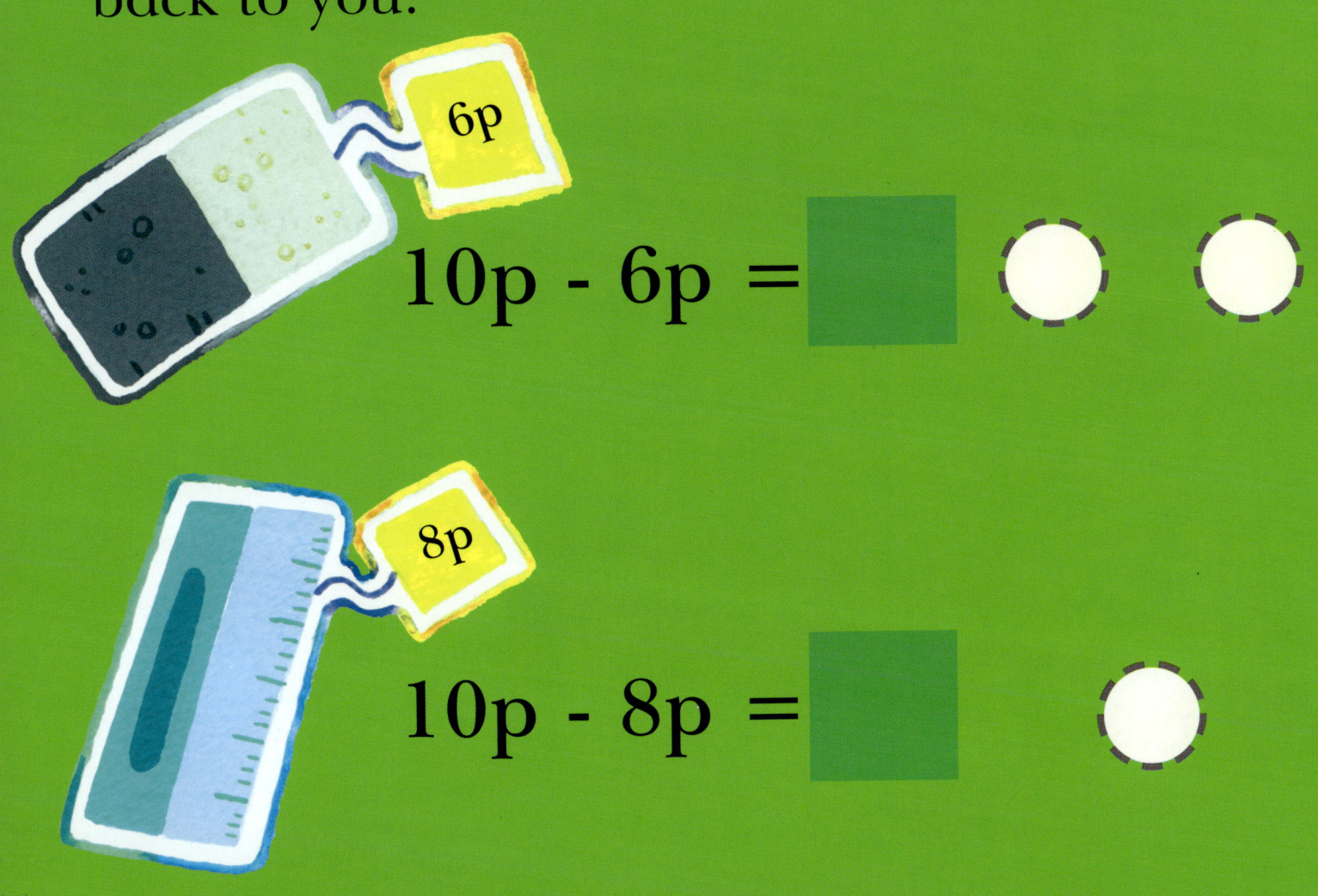

10p - 6p =

10p - 8p =

10p - 6p =   10p - 8p =

You have 20p. Write how much change is left when you buy each of these badges.

20p - 10p =

20p - 18p =

Complete these sums.

20p - 10p =   20p - 18p =

Find some sticker coins to make up the amount of change that the shopkeeper gives back to you.

20p - 17p =

20p - 11p =

20p - 17p =   20p - 11p =

You have 50p. Write how much change is left when you buy each of these fruits.

50p - 20p =

50p - 30p =

Complete these sums.

50p - 20p =   50p - 30p =

Find some sticker coins to make up the amount of change that the shopkeeper gives back to you.

50p - 45p =

50p - 25p =

Add some more coins to each box to make up the price of each vegetable.

Complete these sums.

20p + ☐ = 30p   20p + ☐ = 40p